A Note to Teachers & Parents
from the Author...

I've written the SmartStart Guitar method and this SmartStart Songbook hoping that you will pick up a guitar and find your way around with ease. With just a few simple finger positions (chords) you can play any song in this book, and sing along. You can play guitar in "SmartStart G" as long as you like, or make a smooth transition into standard tuning with the method book when your playing begins to feel completely natural. And it will, if you play regularly.

In case you're shy about singing with people, I encourage you to give it a go. Singing together really feels good and has been known to reduce daily stress and promote general well-being. Even if you're someone who sometimes finds it hard to hear where to begin, you can start out by singing along with the enclosed CD. You'll find the first singing note of each song at the top of every page.

If you're considering making music with children, you can rest assured that they are a most forgiving and appreciative audience. Your beginning guitar skills and a "shower singer's" rendition of any favorite song will garner their applause. I play music with kids every day and find that helping them discover their own creativity is one of life's greatest joys. In that spirit, these songs correspond with popular educational themes for students in pre-school through the elementary grades. Some of these songs are serious, others just plain silly. Together, they tell the story of America and her diverse, imaginative, and courageous people. I hope they'll make everyone's learning experiences memorable, and inspire children's pride in this country where we are free to sing about real life and grow our own dreams.

Thank you for keeping traditional music alive!

Jessica Baron Turner

The SmartStart Guitar Songbook

Songs marked with an asterisk can be appropriate for any grade, including preschool.

ABOUT SMARTSTART GUITAR TUNING

- This book contains songs that have been arranged in "SmartStart G" tuning because it makes the guitar easier to play right away. Strumming the open strings in "SmartStart G" tuning IS the G chord.

- You can play these songs in standard tuning, too with the regular G, D, C, and Em chords. You can also transpose these songs out of "SmartStart G" into any key for standard tuning using the SmartStart Transposition Wheel (see page 7.)

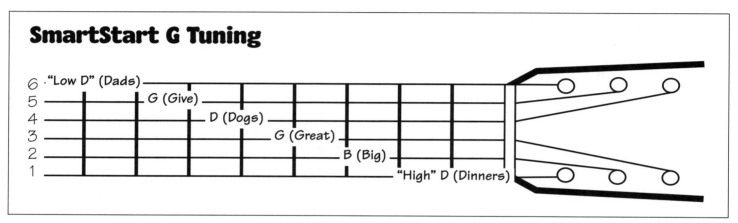

SmartStart G Tuning

6 — "Low D" (Dads)
5 — G (Give)
4 — D (Dogs)
3 — G (Great)
2 — B (Big)
1 — "High" D (Dinners)

Dads **G**ive **D**ogs **G**reat **B**ig **D**inners

- The letter names of the strings in SmartStart G Tuning are D, G, D, G, B, D.
- Tune each string to the correct note by matching it with the sound on the recording, a pitch pipe, tuner, or a piano.
- Begin tuning at the sixth string and work up to the first string.
- Take your time. Listen closely.
- Here are the chord charts for playing in "SmartStart G" tuning.

●Easy D

Easy D

strings: 6 5 4 3 2 1
X X O

M P

- An 'x' means don't play that string.
- An 'o' means play the open string.
- A dot means put your finger here.
- The letter tells you which finger to put on the dot.

- Put the tip of your first finger (Pointer) on the second string, between the nut and the first fret. This finger is "in the first fret."
- Put the tip of your second finger (Middle Man) on the third string between the first and second frets. This finger is "in the second fret."
- Strum the top four strings (strings 1-4) and listen. You are playing Easy D, your second chord! Even when you strum all six strings, the chord sounds pretty.

Easy C

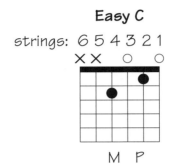

Easy C

strings: 6 5 4 3 2 1

M   P

- First, play Easy D.
- Next take your second finger (Middle Man) off the third string.
- Move Middle Man to the fourth string and keep it in the second fret.
- Strum down across the strings and listen to Easy C!
- To play a full C chord, add Ring Lady (the third finger) to the first string in the second fret.

Em

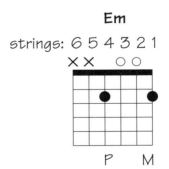

Em

strings: 6 5 4 3 2 1

P   M

- Place Pointer on the fourth string in the second fret.
- Now, place Middle Man on the first string in the second fret.
- When your fingers are curved, press down with your fingertips and strum (strings 1-4 only). You are playing E minor, which is written "Em."
- You can also play Em using the Middle Finger in Pointer's position and Ring Finger in Middle Finger's old position when changing between Em and Easy C.

Intermediate D

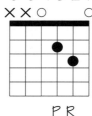

Intermediate D

strings: 6 5 4 3 2 1

P R

- Begin by playing Em.
- Lift Middle Man off of the first string.
- Now put Ring Lady on the second string, in the *third* fret.
- Now strum Intermediate D!

Standard Tuning

If you can comfortably play songs with all of the SmartStart "Easy" and "Intermediate" chords, your hands are ready to learn to play songs in standard tuning with standard chords. You'll be developing more hand strength, flexibility and coordination, so please be kind to yourself and your fingers as you learn. As with anything else, practice will promote success.

To learn more about playing guitar in standard tuning, first tune your guitar in standard tuning and play the Easy C chord. When played in standard tuning, this becomes an A minor 7 chord, (written Am7). To continue along the recommended course of SmartStart Guitar instruction, please refer to the SmartStart Guitar method book.

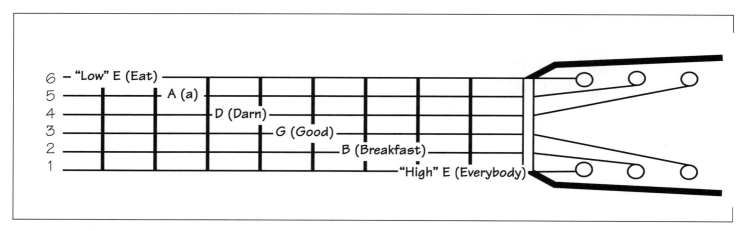

- Get your pitch pipe, tuner, or go to a piano.
- Tune the sixth string up from "low" D to "low" E.
- Tune the first string up from "high" D to "high" E.
- Tune the fifth string up from G to A.
- Check the pitches of strings 4 (D), 3 (G), and 2 (B) to be sure they are still in tune.

THE SMARTSTART GUITAR TRANSPOSITION WHEEL

If you'd like to transpose any song from "SmartStart G" tuning to a new key in standard tuning, take a trip around this wheel to find the identity of each new chord. You can also create new SmartStart Guitar arrangements for songs not found in this book by transposing them out of standard tuning into "SmartStart G" tuning. Once you understand this transposition wheel, you can write it out for yourself anywhere, anytime and transpose songs in just a moment.

SmartStart

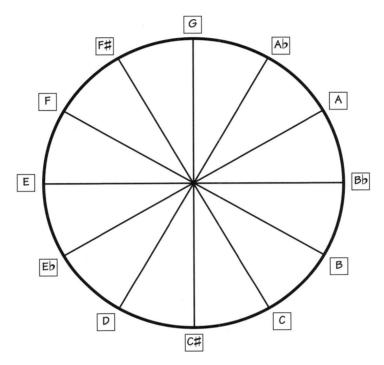

1. Every letter (chord name) on the wheel is one station or musical "half step" away from the chord before it and the one behind it.
2. Begin by finding "G" on the wheel. This represents the key of "SmartStart G."
3. Next, find the name of the key you'd like to transpose to.
4. Now, count and remember how many half-step positions lie clockwise between "G" and the new key. (Example: To transpose from G to B♭ travel clockwise 3 half-step positions around the wheel.)
5. To transpose any other chord, find its position on the wheel. Then, travel the same number of half-steps clockwise as you did to transpose that first "G" chord. Whichever letter you land on is the chord you need to play in the new key. (Example: Transposing from G to B♭; G changes to B♭; D changes to F; C changes to E♭; Em changes to Gm.)

SmartStart Strums

In the SmartStart Guitar method book for children, you'll find instructions for playing:

- **6** • The Marching Strum   (Down, Down, Down, Down)
- **7** • The Horseback Strum   (Do-own, up, Do-own, up)
- **8** • The Two Step Strum   (Pluck, Down, Pluck, Down)
- **9** • The Waltz Strum   (Down, Down, Down)
- **10** • The Three Step Strum   (Pluck, Down, Down, Pluck, Down,Down)

In the SmartStart Guitar method book for beginning adults, you can learn even more strums.

To play the songs in this book with more variety, try these three new strums!

- **11** • **The Boom-Chicka Strum** (Down, rest, Down, Up)

  This strum has a sequence of four steady beats and goes along with its title.
  - On the first beat, strum down across all the strings with a flatpick.
  - On the second beat, pause or "rest."
  - On the third beat, strum down again.
  - On the final beat, strum back up from strings 1-4.

- **12** • **The Cowboy Strum** (Pluck, rest, Down, Up)

  This strum should lope along lazily like a slow horseback ride. The first and third beats in the sequence are long. The second and the fourth beats are very short. So the cadence is "lo-o-ong, short(rest), lo-o-ong, short."
  - On the first beat, pluck the 6th, 5th, OR 4th string with your thumb or flatpick.
  - On the second beat, pause or "rest."
  - On the third beat, strum down across strings 4-1. (To strum down using your fingers, drag the backs of your fingernails lightly across the strings.)
  - On the final beat, strum back up across strings 1-4. (To strum up with your fingers, drag the tip of your pointer finger across the strings.)

Reading Your Musical Charts
SmartStart Guitar's New Presentation of Music

Your new SmartStart Guitar musical charts feature a new, more convenient lay-out developed for people with a strong "visual" learning style.

Suggested Strums:

In the upper left hand corner of each song chart, you'll find one or more suggested strums. These are for your convenience, but other strums or picking patterns wil also work. To remember how to play the suggested strums, please turn to page 8 or refer to your SmartStart Guitar method book.

Chords for Each Song:

Under the suggested strums is a list of the all the chords in the song. This information lets you scan the book for songs you are ready to play. Sometimes a chord is optional. If you don't want to play it, just ignore the chord symbol in the music. String these chords together in any order to create a great warm-up exercise before you begin putting the music and lyrics together.

First Singing Note:

If you'd like to hear the first singing note of a song before you begin singing, pluck the correct note in the indicated position, and match your voice to it. If you're playing with a capo, pluck the same finger and string position indicated but find the new fret position to the right of your capo, as if the capo were the nut of the guitar.

Capo Positions:

If a song played in "SmartStart G" is out of children's normal vocal range, a capo position has been recommended to make the key more suitable for singing. Most often, the suggested capo position is on the third or the fifth fret. Playing SmartStart chords with a capo at the third fret allows you to play chords you already know and be able to sing in the key of Bb. Playing with the capo at the fifth fret allows you to play and sing songs in the key of C.

Number of Strums Per Chord:

Next to each chord you'll find a number in parentheses. This tells you how many times to play the suggested strum before changing to the next chord. If you play through the song according to the number of strums for each chord, you'll begin to "hear" the music and feel the melodic patterns of each song independent of the lyrics.

Underlined Lyric Syllables:

Some strums require one kind of motion on the first beat (such as a plucking a bass string) followed by a different motion on the next beats in the strum sequence (such as strumming down across the strings.) Syllables or words that fall on the downbeat have been underlined so you can better see when to pluck a bass string or initiate a new strum sequence.

Reader-Friendly Line Breaks:

Wherever possible, SmartStart Guitar charts feature musical line breaks that correspond with completed strumming sequences and chord changes. This has been done to help you keep the flow of your playing while you sing and change chords. Additionally, each new line of music shows you what chord to play at the beginning, even if you were ALREADY playing it on the previous line. This will help you get back on track quickly if you loose your place.

CAPOING UP TO HIGHER KEYS IN SMARTSTART TUNING

No Capo	Capo 1st fret	Capo 2nd fret	Capo 3rd fret	Capo 4th fret	Capo 5th fret	Capo 6th fret	Capo 7th fret
SmartStart G	Ab	A	Bb	B	C	C#	D
Easy D & Int. D	Eb	E	F	F#	G	Ab	A
Easy C	C#	D	Eb	E	F	F#	G
Em	Fm	F#m	Gm	Abm	Am	Bbm	Bm

⟐ AMERICA ("MY COUNTRY 'TIS OF THEE")

Marching Strum, slowly with dignity
Chords: SmartStart G, Easy D, Easy C
First Singing Note: G, 3rd string, open
Capo Position: 3rd Fret

Lyrics by Samuel F. Smith
Music by Henry Carey

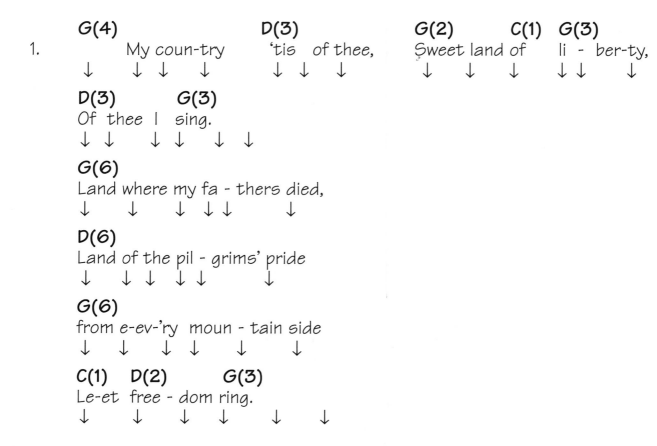

1.
G(4)   D(3)   G(2)   C(1) G(3)
My coun-try   'tis of thee,   Sweet land of li - ber-ty,
↓   ↓ ↓   ↓   ↓ ↓ ↓   ↓   ↓   ↓   ↓ ↓   ↓

D(3)   G(3)
Of thee I sing.
↓ ↓   ↓ ↓   ↓ ↓

G(6)
Land where my fa - thers died,
↓   ↓   ↓   ↓ ↓   ↓

D(6)
Land of the pil - grims' pride
↓   ↓ ↓ ↓ ↓   ↓

G(6)
from e-ev-'ry moun - tain side
↓   ↓   ↓   ↓   ↓   ↓

C(1) D(2)   G(3)
Le-et free - dom ring.
↓   ↓   ↓   ↓   ↓   ↓

2. My native country thee,
    Land of the noble free,
    Thy name I love.
    I love they rocks and rills,
    Thy woods thy templed hills,
    My heart with rapture thrills
    Like that above.

✦ APPLES AND BANANAS

Marching Strum, Horseback Strum, or Two Step Strum
Capo Position: 5th fret
Chords: SmartStart G, Easy D, Easy C
First Singing Note: B, 2nd string, open

Traditional

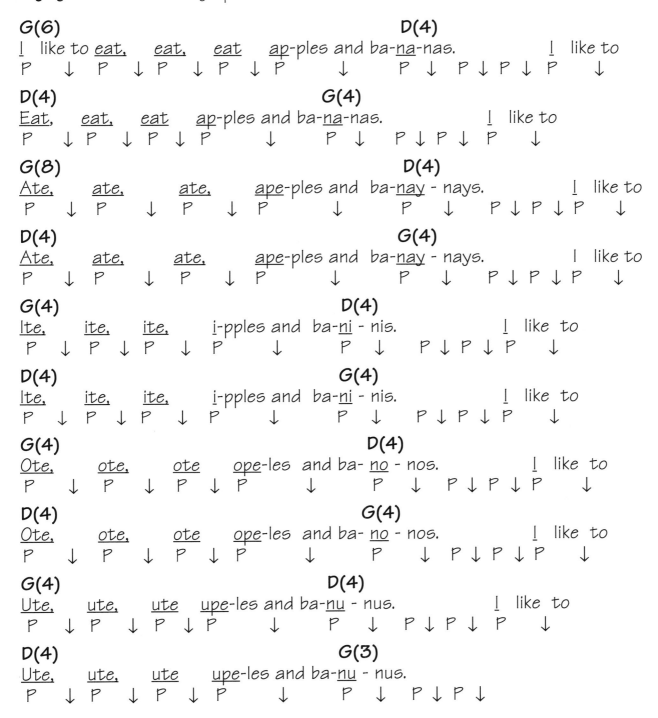

Repeat first verse.

Sign Language: This song lends itself to teaching children the alphabet in sign language. Show children how to sing "a", "e", "i", "o" and "u". Next, ask them to sign each vowel as it occurs in the song. Adding the kinesthetic and visual experience of signing will reinforce children's knowledge of the sequence of the vowels in the song, and it's fun to do.

◆ THE BARNYARD SONG

Two Step Strum   Traditional
Chords: SmartStart G, Easy D optional
First Singing Note: G, 3rd string, open
Capo Position: 5th fret

Strumming Suggestion: Alternate your bass strings by choosing two, and playing first one then strumming down, then the other before strumming down again. Repeat this sequence throughout the song. The 6th string and 4th string make a nice alternating pattern for this song.

    G(8)
1.   I had a <u>cat</u> and the <u>cat</u> pleased <u>me.</u> I <u>fed</u> my <u>cat</u> under <u>yon</u>-der <u>tree.</u>
    P ↓   P ↓   P ↓   P ↓ P ↓ P ↓   P ↓ P ↓

    G(1)   **D(1)**   **G(1)**   **D(1)**   **G(2)**
    <u>Cat</u> goes <u>fid-dle</u> - i -<u>fee,</u>   <u>fid-dle</u> - i - <u>fee!</u>
    P   ↓   P   ↓ P ↓ P   ↓ P ↓ P ↓

    G(8)
2.   I had a <u>hen</u>, the <u>hen</u> pleased <u>me</u>,   I <u>fed</u> my <u>hen</u> under <u>yon</u>-der <u>tree.</u> The
    P ↓ P   ↓ P ↓   P ↓P ↓ P ↓   P ↓ P   ↓

    G(3)
    <u>Hen</u> goes <u>chim-my</u> chuck, <u>chim-my</u> chuck,
    P   ↓   P   ↓   P   ↓

    G(1)   **D(1)**   **G(1)**   **D(1)**   **G(4)**
    <u>Cat</u> goes <u>fid-dle</u>- i - <u>fee,</u>   <u>fid-dle</u> - i - <u>fee!</u>
    P   ↓   P   ↓ P ↓ P   ↓ P ↓ P ↓ P ↓ P ↓

3.   Duck... quacky, quacky

4.   Hog... griffy gruffy

5.   Sheep... baaa, baaa

6.   Goose... swishy, swashy

7.   Cow... mooo, mooo

8.   Dog... bow-wow, bow-wow

9.   Horse... neigh, neigh

⑯ THE BOLL WEEVIL

Two Step Strum or Cowboy Strum, lightly   Traditional
Chords: SmartStart G, Easy D, Easy C
First Singing Note: D, 1st string, open
Capo Position: 7th fret

In 1892, Texas cotton farmers were the first to report the bad news about the boll weevil, a little bug that ruined their crops and spread all over the south, destroying cotton fields as they went. As the song tells, many farmers lost their farms, homes, and fortunes when the boll weevil came along.

1.   **G(8)**
The boll wee-vil is a lit-tle black bug, come from Mex-i - co they say.   Came
         P   ↓   P ↓ P   ↓   P   ↓   P   ↓ P ↓ P ↓ P ↓

        C(4)   **G(4)**
All the way to Tex-as   just a-look-in' for a place to stay. Just a-look-in' for a
P   ↓ P   ↓ P ↓ P ↓   P   ↓   P   ↓ P   ↓   P   ↓

        D(4)   **G(4)**
Home…   just a-look-in' for a home…
P   ↓ P ↓ P ↓ P   ↓   P ↓ P ↓ P ↓ P ↓

2.   The first time I saw that weevil, he was sittin' on the square
        The next time I saw him he had all his family there.
        Just a-lookin' for a home… just a-lookin' for a home.

3.   The Boll Weevil said to the Farmer, "You better leave me alone.
        I done et up all your cotton, now I'm starting on your corn.
        Gonna make myself a home… Gonna make myself a home.

4.   Well, the Merchant got half the cotton, The Boll Weevils got the rest.
        Didn't leave the poor Farmer's wife but one old cotton dress,
        And it's full of holes… all full of holes.

5.   The last time I saw that weevil, he was settled down for life;
        He'd brought has aunts and uncles, his cousins and his wife.
        Just a-lookin' for a home… just a-lookin' for a home.

❖ CAPE COD CHANTEY

Two Step Strum
Chords: SmartStart G, Easy D, Easy C
First Singing Note: B, 2nd string, open
Capo Position: None

Traditional New England Sea Chantey

       G(6)
1.   <u>Cape</u> Cod <u>girls</u> they <u>have</u> no <u>combs.</u>
    P   ↓   P   ↓   P   ↓   P   ↓

       G(2)   **D(2)**
    Heave a-<u>way,</u>   Heave a-<u>way!</u> They
    P   ↓   P   ↓   P   ↓   P   ↓ P ↓

       G(4)
    <u>Comb</u> their <u>hair</u> with <u>cod</u>-fish <u>bones.</u>
    P   ↓   P   ↓   P   ↓   P

       G(2)   **D(1)**   **G(1)**
    We are <u>bound</u> for   Aus-<u>tra</u> - li - a!
    ↓   P   ↓   P   ↓   P   ↓   P ↓

       G(4)
Chorus: <u>Heave</u> a-<u>way</u> my <u>bul</u>-ly, bul-ly boys,
    P   ↓   P   ↓ P   ↓   P   ↓

       G(2)   **D(1)**
    Heave a-<u>way,</u>   Heave a-<u>way!</u>
    P   ↓   P   ↓   P   ↓   P   ↓

       G(4)
    <u>Heave</u> a-<u>way</u> and <u>don't</u> you make a <u>noise,</u>
    P   ↓P   ↓ P   ↓   P

       G(2)   **D(1)**   **G(1)**
    We are <u>bound</u> for   Aus-<u>tra</u> - li - a!
    ↓   P   ↓   P   ↓   P   ↓   P ↓

       G(6)
2.   <u>Cape</u> Cod <u>boys</u> they <u>have</u> no <u>sleds,</u>
    P   ↓ P   ↓ P   ↓ P   ↓

       G(3)   **D(1)**
    Heave a-<u>way,</u>   Heave a-<u>way!</u>   They
    P   ↓ P   ↓   P   ↓ P   ↓

       G(4)
    <u>Slide</u> down <u>hill</u> on <u>cod</u>-fish <u>heads,</u>
    P   ↓   P ↓P   ↓ P

       G(2)   **D(1)**   **G(1)**
    We are <u>bound</u> for   Aus-<u>tra</u> - li - a!
    ↓   P   ↓   P   ↓   P   ↓   P ↓

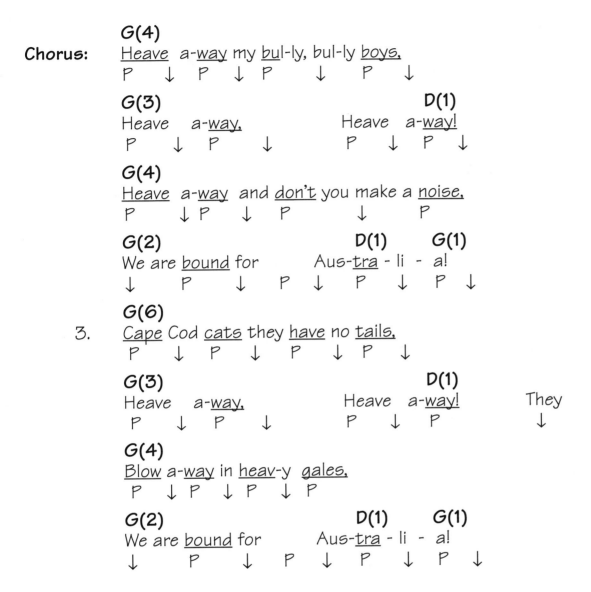

Chorus:

G(4)
Heave a-way my bul-ly, bul-ly boys,
P ↓ P ↓ P ↓ P ↓

G(3)   D(1)
Heave a-way,   Heave a-way!
P ↓ P ↓   P ↓ P ↓

G(4)
Heave a-way and don't you make a noise,
P ↓ P ↓ P ↓ P

G(2)   D(1)   G(1)
We are bound for   Aus-tra - li - a!
↓ P ↓ P ↓ P ↓ P ↓

G(6)
3.   Cape Cod cats they have no tails,
P ↓ P ↓ P ↓ P ↓

G(3)   D(1)
Heave a-way,   Heave a-way!   They
P ↓ P ↓   P ↓ P   ↓

G(4)
Blow a-way in heav-y gales,
P ↓ P ↓ P ↓ P

G(2)   D(1)   G(1)
We are bound for   Aus-tra - li - a!
↓ P ↓ P ↓ P ↓ P ↓

Singing Parts: This is a fun song for children to sing in single gender groups. In verse one, the girls sing about the boys. In verse two, the boys sing about the girls. Then everyone sings together. They can add rhythmic hand over hand motions of pulling up the anchor and raising the sails to sing this as it was sung a hundred years ago on ships.

◆18 CASEY JONES

Horseback, Two Step Strum or Boom-Chicka Strum
Chords: SmartStart G, Easy D
First Singing Note: G, 3rd string, open
Capo Position: None

This song was written in 1909, just nine years after Casey Jones, a train engineer from Kentucky, tragically crashed the Illinois Central Cannonball into another train in Vaughan, Mississippi. He was killed by steam vapors at the young age of twenty-six. Railroading at the turn of the century was a dangerous occupation, and songs like this one helped memorialize its brave workers during during the industrial age when they were very much needed.

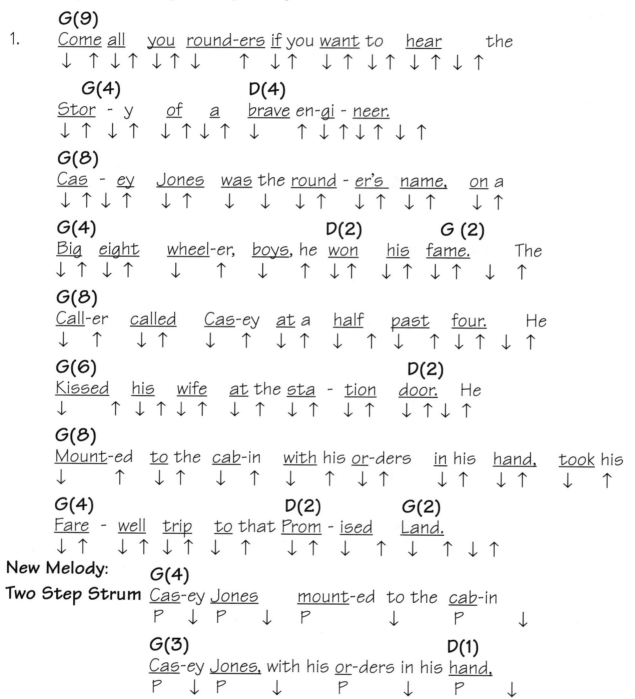

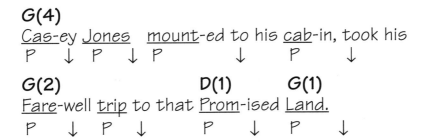

G(4)
<u>Cas</u>-ey <u>Jones</u>   <u>mount</u>-ed to his <u>cab</u>-in, took his
P   ↓   P   ↓   P   ↓   P   ↓

G(2)   **D(1)**   **G(1)**
<u>Fare</u>-well <u>trip</u> to that <u>Prom</u>-ised <u>Land.</u>
P   ↓   P   ↓   P   ↓   P   ↓

2. Casey pulled up to that Reno Hill.
    He whistled for the crossing with an awful shrill.
    The switchman knew by the engine's moan
    That the man at the throttle was Casey Jones.
    He looked at his water and the water was low;
    He looked at his watch and his watch was slow;
    He turned to his fireman and this is what he said,
    "Jim we're gonna reach Frisco but we'll all be dead."
            Casey Jones... gonna reach Frisco
            Casey Jones... but we'll all be dead, etc.

3. Put in your water and shovel your coal;
    Stick your head out the window, watch those drivers roll;
    I'll drive her til she leaves the rail,
    Cause I'm eight hours late with the western mail.
    When he was within six miles of the place
    The number four stared him right in the face.
    He turned to his fireman, said "Jim you'd better jump
    Cause there's two locomotives that are going to bump.
            Casey Jones... two locomotives,
            Casey Jones... going to bump, etc.

4. Casey said just before he died,
    "There's two more trains I'd like to ride."
    The fireman said, "Which ones would they be?"
    "The Northern Pacific and the Santa Fe."
    Mrs. Jones sat on her bed a-sighing,
    Just to hear that her Casey was a-dying.
    "Go to bed children, and hush your cryin'
    Cause you've got another papa on the Salt Lake Line."
            Casey Jones... got another papa
            Casey Jones... on the Salt Lake Line, etc.

19

◆19 CHANUKAH IS HERE

Traditional Melody
Words by Jessica Baron Turner

Marching Strum or Two Step Strum
Chords: SmartStart G, Easy D
First Singing Note: B, 2nd string, open
Capo Position: 5th fret

G(4)
1.   One pret-ty, two pret-ty, three pretty cand-les,
    ↓   ↓   ↓   ↓

D(4)
Four pretty, five pret-ty, six pret-ty cand-les,
    ↓   ↓   ↓   ↓

G(4)   D(2)   G(2)
Sev-en pret-ty, eight pret-ty, nine pret-ty cand-les! Cha-nu-kah is here.
    ↓   ↓   ↓   ↓   ↓   ↓   ↓   ↓

2.   Light each flame with the one in the middle.
    Light each flame with the one in the middle.
    Light each flame with the one in the middle.
    Shamus is its name.

3.   Every candle lights the darkness
    Every candle lights the darkness
    Every candle lights the darkness
    Bringing hope and joy!

4.   We give thanks when we light the menorah.
    We give thanks when we light the menorah.
    We give thanks when we light the menorah.
    For the miracle of light. Repeat verse one

Learning About Chanukah: Chanukah is the winter holiday when Jews celebrate the miracle that occurred when Judah Maccabee and his brothers restored the Jewish temple in Jerusalem over 2300 years ago. The holy place had been vandalized by Syrians who wanted everyone to worship the Greek Gods. When Juda went to light the eternal light, he could find only a tiny jug of oil...just enough for one day. The miracle is that the oil burned for eight days and nights until more could be brought. You can sing this Chanukah song to the tune of "Ten Little Indians," and use your hands to make the "candles" of the menorah. Raise your open hands side by side, palms facing out to create a "menorah." Press your thumbs together in the middle to make the shamus candle. Let your hands help you tell the story as you sing.

CHILD OF GOD

Marching Strum, Gently or **Boom Chicka Strum**
Chords: SmartStart G, Easy D, Easy C, Em
First Singing Note: B, 2nd string, open
Capo Position: 3rd Fret

By Jessica Baron Turner

This song was written in memory of Winona Williams-Burns, an African-American professor who taught children about art and African culture, and taught Child Development at California State University, Northridge.

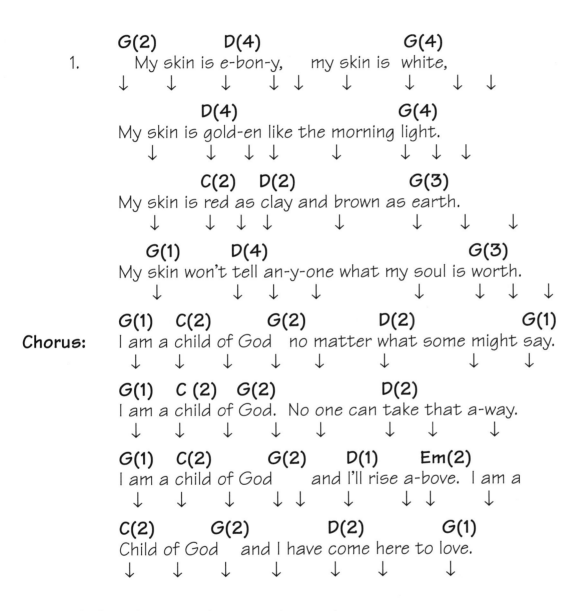

2.   No harsh or careless words can hurt me now.
      I've found the strength in my heart to stand up tall and proud
      And when I look into your eyes I see
      That in your heart of hearts you're a child like me.

♦ DE COLORES

Three Step Strum
Traditional Mexican
Chords: SmartStart G, Easy D, Easy C
First Singing Note: D, 1st string, open
Capo Position: None

In this pretty Mexican song, the first verse describes the colors of Spring, the birds, and a rainbow. In the chorus, the singer says she is like the beautiful colors of spring. Verse two tells of the rooster, the hen, their chicks, and the cheerful sounds they all make.

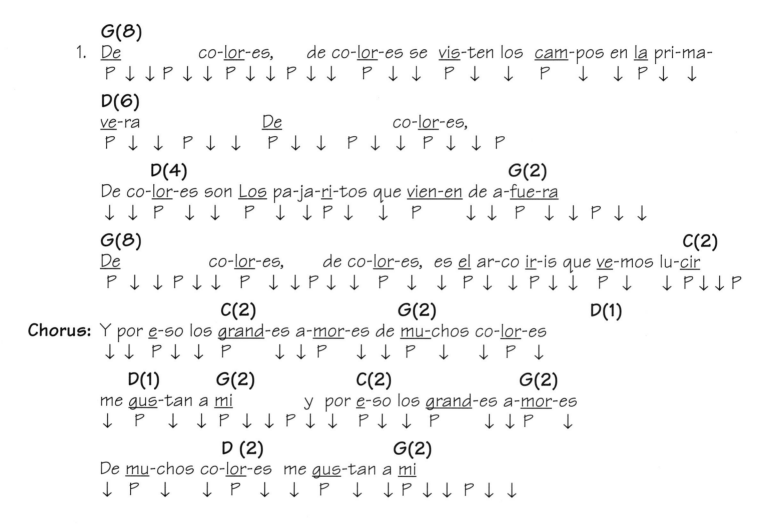

2. Canta el gallo, canta el gallo con el kiri, kiri, kiri, kiri, kiri
   La *gadina*, la gadina con el kara, kara, kara, kara, kara
   Los *polluetos*, los polluetos con el pio, pio, pio, pio, pi

✦ DOWN BY THE RIVERSIDE

Horseback Strum, Two Step Strum or Cowboy Strum, lively   Traditional Spiritual
Chords: SmartStart G, Easy D, Easy C
First Singing Note: B, 2nd string, open
Capo Position: 3rd fret

Backbeat Rhythm: This song features a "back beat" rhythm. Emphasis belongs on the second and fourth beat in each group of four beats. You can get a feel for playing the back beat if you whisper "one" and clap on "two", whisper "three" and clap on "four."

This song dates back long before the Viet Nam war, but it was sung a great deal by American protestors who wanted to see President Nixon help bring end the conflict.

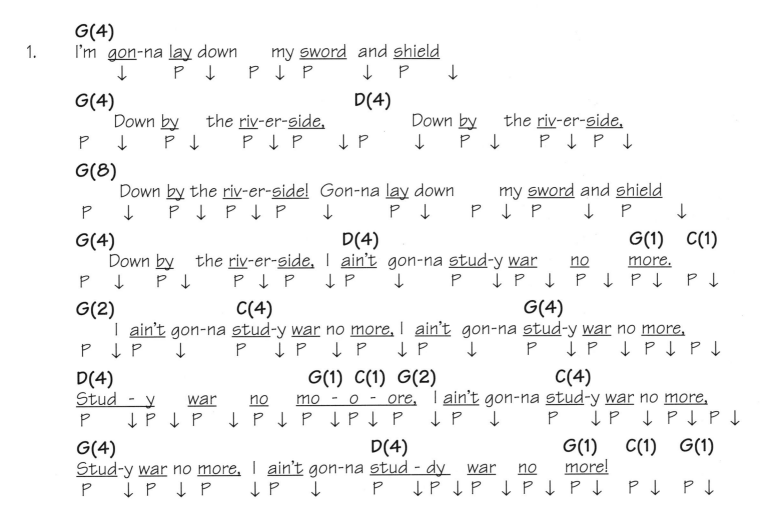

2.   Gonna walk with the Prince of Peace...

3.   Gonna shake hands with everyone...

4.   Gonna make friends around the world...

❖ EVERYBODY'S GARDEN

Horseback Strum or Cowboy Strum
Chords: SmartStart G, Easy D optional, Easy C optional
First Singing Note: G, 3rd string, open
Capo Position: 2nd fret

Traditional Melody
Lyrics by Jessica Baron Turner

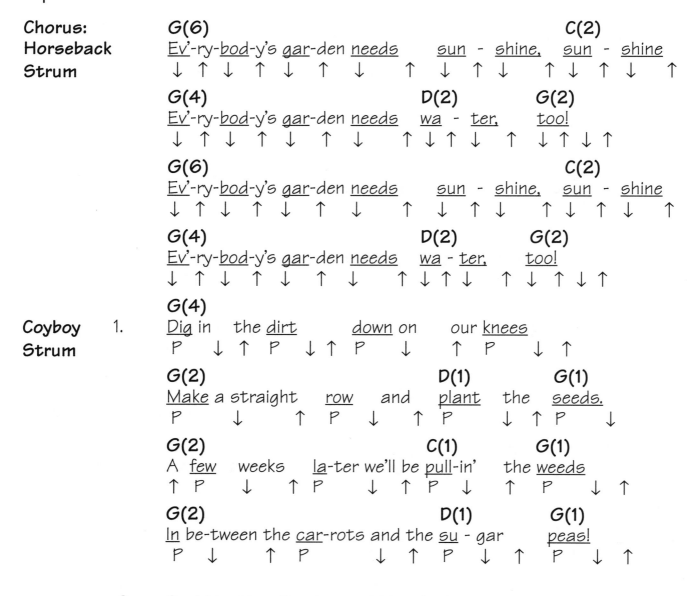

Chorus:
Horseback Strum

G(6)   C(2)
Ev'-ry-bod-y's gar-den needs   sun - shine, sun - shine
↓ ↑ ↓ ↑ ↓ ↑ ↓   ↑ ↓ ↑ ↓   ↑ ↓ ↑ ↓   ↑

G(4)   D(2)   G(2)
Ev'-ry-bod-y's gar-den needs   wa - ter,   too!
↓ ↑ ↓ ↑ ↓ ↑ ↓   ↑ ↓ ↑ ↓   ↑ ↓ ↑ ↓ ↑

G(6)   C(2)
Ev'-ry-bod-y's gar-den needs   sun - shine, sun - shine
↓ ↑ ↓ ↑ ↓ ↑ ↓   ↑ ↓ ↑ ↓   ↑ ↓ ↑ ↓   ↑

G(4)   D(2)   G(2)
Ev'-ry-bod-y's gar-den needs   wa - ter,   too!
↓ ↑ ↓ ↑ ↓ ↑ ↓   ↑ ↓ ↑ ↓   ↑ ↓ ↑ ↓ ↑

Cowboy Strum   1.

G(4)
Dig in   the dirt   down on   our knees
P ↓ ↑ P ↓ ↑ P ↓   ↑ P   ↓ ↑

G(2)   D(1)   G(1)
Make a straight   row   and   plant   the   seeds.
P   ↓   ↑ P ↓   ↑ P   ↓ ↑ P   ↓

G(2)   C(1)   G(1)
A few   weeks   la-ter we'll be pull-in'   the weeds
↑ P   ↓   ↑ P   ↓ ↑ P ↓   ↑   P   ↓ ↑

G(2)   D(1)   G(1)
In be-tween the car-rots and the su - gar   peas!
P   ↓   ↑ P   ↓ ↑ P ↓ ↑ P   ↓ ↑

2.   Could be the climate, could be the love…
     Could be the rain that falls from above.
     It might be magic, and it may be luck
     But there's a bushel full of beans on the back of my truck

Science: What other kinds of fruit and vegetables besides carrots and beans might be in the bushel on the back of your truck? This song will give you an opportunity to help students discuss what kinds of produce are grown in your vicinity, and which ones are brought in from far away.

Language Arts: What fruits and vegetables rhyme with or sound similar to "seeds?" You can teach these concepts as well as poetic meter by replacing sugar peas in verse two with something new. (Hint: "berries" work well!)

◆ THE FARMER IN THE DELL

Horseback Strum, walking pace
Chords: SmartStart G, Easy D optional
First Singing Note: D, 4th string, open
Capo Position: 3rd fret

Traditional Melody
Lyric Adaptations by Jessica Baron Turner

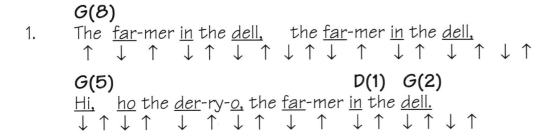

1. The far-mer in the dell,   the far-mer in the dell,

   Hi,   ho the der-ry-o, the far-mer in the dell.

2. The farmer takes a wife (or husband)…

3. The couple takes a child…

4. The child takes a dog…

5. The dog takes a cat…

6. The cat takes a mouse…

7. The mouse takes the cheese…

8. The cheese takes a bow…

Musical Game: Invite the children to circle up and hold hands. Ask one child to stand in the center of the circle to be "The Farmer." The children in the circle walk around to their right singing verse one of the song. When it ends, they stop and the farmer chooses one of them to be his wife or her husband. The circling and singing begin again for each verse and stop only while the children in the center build their group. Once the mouse takes the cheese, all the other children leave the "Cheese" in the middle and join the outer circle. The Cheese takes his or her bow in the center, then becomes the new "Farmer" as the game begins again. This version of the game eliminates the cheese having to stand alone because of its pungeont odor. It can bow with pride instead.

◈ THE FARMER IS THE MAN

Marching Strum, Two Step Strum or Cowboy Strum, lightly
Chords: SmartStart G, easy D, Easy C, Em optional
First Singing Note: G, 3rd string, open
Capo Position: 3rd fret

Traditional

Farming has always been a hard way for people to make a living, but we depend on farmers for our fruit, grains, and vegetables.
Farmers know the land, the soil, and the seasons better than anyone, because their crops depend on them.

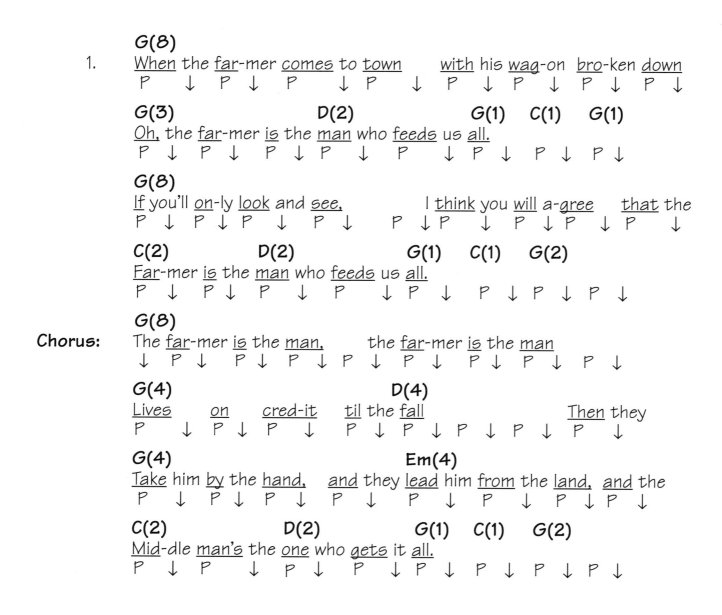

2.   When the lawyer hangs around and the butcher cuts a pound
     The farmer is the man who feeds them all.
     And the preacher and the cook go a-strolling by the brook,
     But the farmer is the man who feeds them all.
     The farmer is the man, the farmer is the man lives on credit til the fall
     With the interest rate so high, it's a wonder he don't die,
     For the mortgage man's the one who gets it all.

3.   When the banker says he's broke and the merchant's up in smoke
     They forget that it's the farmer feeds them all.
     It would put them to the test if the farmer took a rest,
     Then they'd know that it's the farmer feeds them all.
     The farmer is the man, the farmer is the man lives on credit til the fall.
     And his pants are wearing thin, his condition it's a sin,
     He's forgot that he's the man who feeds us all.

◈26 GIT ALONG LITTLE DOGIES

Waltz Strum, Three Step Strum or Double Cowboy Strum
Chords: SmartStart G, Easy D, Easy C. Em optional
First Singing Note: D, 1st string, open
Capo Position: 3rd fret

Traditional Western

Between 1870 and 1890, cowboys drove twelve million "do-gies" meaning "cows" up from Texas to Wyoming. These trips were long, dusty, and hard on people and animals alike. When the cattle got hornery and restless on the trail ("fiery and snuffy") each one could be a thousand pounds of dangerous and unpredictable! Sometimes cowboys would gently call out "Whoopie ti-yi-yo" to calm them down.

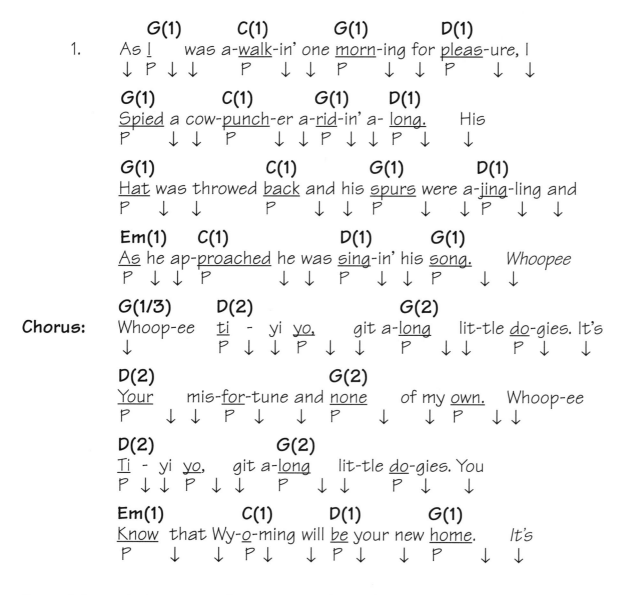

```
              G(1)        C(1)        G(1)         D(1)
  1.    As I    was a-walk-in' one morn-ing for pleas-ure, I
         ↓  P  ↓  ↓     P    ↓  ↓  P    ↓  ↓  P   ↓   ↓

        G(1)        C(1)        G(1)      D(1)
        Spied a cow-punch-er a-rid-in' a- long.      His
        P     ↓  ↓   P    ↓  ↓ P  ↓  ↓ P  ↓    ↓

        G(1)              C(1)         G(1)           D(1)
        Hat was thrown back and his spurs were a-jing-ling and
        P   ↓   ↓        P    ↓  ↓  P    ↓  ↓ P   ↓  ↓

        Em(1)    C(1)              D(1)       G(1)
        As he ap-proached he was sing-in' his song.     Whoopee
        P  ↓  ↓  P          ↓  ↓  P   ↓  ↓  P   ↓  ↓

        G(1/3)     D(2)                   G(2)
Chorus: Whoop-ee   ti - yi yo,      git a-long    lit-tle do-gies. It's
         ↓         P  ↓  ↓ P ↓  ↓     P    ↓  ↓    P  ↓    ↓

        D(2)                 G(2)
        Your    mis-for-tune and none    of my own.   Whoop-ee
        P    ↓  ↓   P   ↓   ↓  P   ↓   ↓ P  ↓  ↓

        D(2)              G(2)
        Ti - yi yo,    git a-long    lit-tle do-gies. You
        P ↓ ↓ P ↓ ↓     P   ↓  ↓     P  ↓    ↓

        Em(1)         C(1)       D(1)      G(1)
        Know  that Wy-o-ming will be your new home.      It's
        P     ↓    ↓ P↓    ↓ P↓   ↓  P ↓    ↓
```

2.   It's early in spring that we round up the dogies
      We mark them and brand them and bob off their tails
      We round up our horses, load up the chuck wagon
      And then throw the dogies out onto the trail.

♦ GREEN GROW THE RUSHES-O

Marching Strum or Two Step Strum, Quickly and Lightly　　　　Traditional, Ireland
Chords: SmartStart G, Easy D , Eas y C
First Singing Note: G, 1st string, 5th fret
Capo Position: 7th fret

This song may be derived from the Jewish holiday, Passover, when the question is asked, "Who knoweth thirteen?" The prayer offers thirteen responses ending with "One is God alone. Which is over Heaven and Earth." This song includes many religious symbols from the New Testament (Christian) and so is also associated with Easter, which comes at the same time of year as Passover.

3.　　Three for the rivals...
4.　　Four for the Gospel makers...
5.　　Five for the symbols at your door...
6.　　Six for the six proud walkers...
7.　　Seven for the seven stars in the sky...
8.　　Eight for the April rainers...
9.　　Nine for the nine bright shiners...
10.　Ten for the Ten Commandments...
11.　Eleven for the eleven that went to heaven...
12.　Twelve for the Twelve Apostles...

◆28 HARD TIMES, COME AGAIN NO MORE

Marching Strum, gently   By Stephen Foster
Chords: SmartStart G, Easy D, Easy C
First Singing Note: G, 3rd string, open
Capo Position: None

Quick Change Challenge: This song gives you great opportunities to practice quick chord changes between G and C chords.

Stephen Foster wrote this and many other powerful songs in the 1800s. Although Americans have always known poverty and suffering, the Great Depression after the 1929 stock market crash sent many citizens into poverty. This song gained added popularity during that time, and remains a favorite.

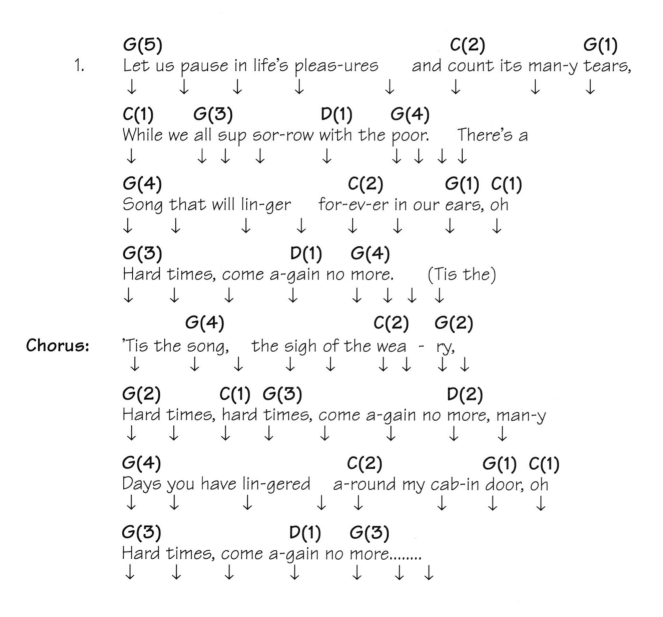

2. While we seek the mirth and beauty and music light and gay,
    There are frail forms fainting at the door.
    Though their voices are silent, their pleading looks will say,
    Oh, hard times, come again no more

3. There's a pale drooping maiden who toils her life away
    With a worn heart whose better days are o'er,
    Though her voice would be merry, 'tis sighing all the day,
    Oh, hard times, come again no more

4. 'Tis a sigh that is wafted across the troubled wave,
    'Tis a wail that is heard upon the shore,
    'Tis a dirge that is murmured around the lowly grave,
    Oh, hard times, come again no more

◆29 HOME ON THE RANGE

Marching Strum, Three Step Strum, or Waltz Strum, lazily
Chords: SmartStart G, Easy D, Easy C, Em optional
First Singing Note: D, 4th string, open
Capo Position: 3rdfret

Traditional, from Kansas

       G(2)   C(2)

1.   Oh <u>give</u> me a <u>home</u>   where the <u>buf</u>-fa-lo <u>roam</u> where the
    ↓ P ↓ ↓ P   ↓ ↓   P ↓ ↓ P ↓ ↓

    G(1)   Em(1)   D(2)

    <u>Deer</u>   and the <u>an</u>-te-lope <u>play</u>   where
    P ↓ ↓   P ↓ ↓   P ↓ ↓   P ↓   ↓

    G(2)   C(2)

    <u>Sel</u>-dom is <u>heard</u>   a dis-<u>cour</u>-ag-ing <u>word</u>   and the
    P ↓   ↓ P   ↓ ↓   P   ↓ ↓   P   ↓ ↓

    G(1)   D(1)   G(1)   D(1)

    <u>Skies</u>   are not <u>cloud</u>-y all <u>day.</u>
    P   ↓   ↓ P   ↓↓P ↓ ↓ P ↓ ↓

Chorus: G(1)   C(1)   G(2)

    <u>Home,</u>   <u>home</u> on the <u>range,</u>   where the
    P   ↓   ↓ P   ↓ ↓   P   ↓ ↓ P ↓↓

    Em(2)   D(2)

    <u>Deer</u> and the <u>an</u>-te-lope <u>play</u>   where
    P ↓ ↓ P ↓ ↓   P ↓ ↓ P ↓ ↓

    G(2)   C(2)

    <u>Sel</u>-dom is <u>heard</u>   a dis-<u>cour</u>-ag-ing <u>word</u>   and the
    P ↓   ↓ P   ↓ ↓   P   ↓ ↓ P   ↓ ↓

    G(1)   D(1)   G(2)

    <u>Skies</u>   are not <u>cloud</u>-y all <u>day.</u>
    P   ↓   ↓ P   ↓ ↓P ↓   ↓ P ↓   ↓

♪ HOT TIME IN THE OLD TOWN TONIGHT

Marching or Two Step Strum, Easily
Traditional
Chords: SmartStart G, Easy D
First Singing Note: B, 2nd string, open
Capo Position: 3rd fret

Although it could never be proven, it is probably true that on the night of October 8, 1871, Mrs. Kate O'Leary's cow started the Chicago fire by kicking a lantern over in her barn fully stocked with hay, and flammable winter supplies. The fire destroyed much of the city and burned the houses of 10,000 people. It began a new era for Chicago because everything had to be rebuilt. The broken lamp that started the fire is rumoured to have survived, but it was never seen again!

A Fast Blast: To have lots of fun with this song, play and sing a little faster each time you repeat the verse!

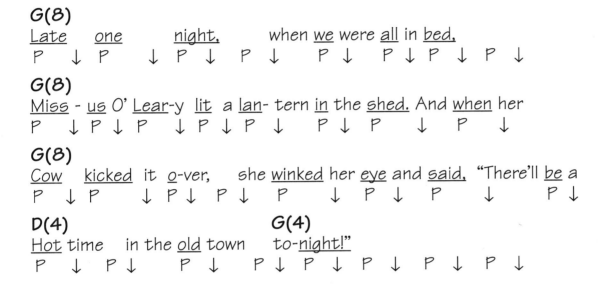

```
G(8)
Late     one      night,       when we were all in bed,
P    ↓  P      ↓  P ↓  P  ↓      P ↓   P ↓ P ↓ P  ↓

G(8)
Miss - us O' Lear-y lit a lan- tern in the shed. And when her
P    ↓ P ↓ P    ↓ P ↓ P ↓    P ↓ P    ↓   P    ↓

G(8)
Cow    kicked it o-ver,     she winked her eye and said, "There'll be a
P   ↓ P    ↓ P ↓ P ↓   P      ↓ P ↓ P   ↓         P ↓

D(4)                        G(4)
Hot time   in the old town   to-night!"
P   ↓ P ↓     P  ↓  P ↓ P ↓ P  ↓ P ↓ P ↓
```

33

♦ I RIDE AN OLD PAINT

Waltz Strum, Three Step Strum or Cowboy Strum, lazily
Chords: SmartStart G, Easy D, Easy C
First Singing Note: D, 4th string, open
Capo Position: 3rd fret

Traditional

Strumming Clue! The lyric begins on the last down strum in a Three Step sequence. The new sequence starts with the word "ride."
The underlined words represent the first beat in each new strum sequence.

```
        G(4)
1.      I   ride   an old Paint,  I'm lead-in' old Dan,  I'm
        ↓   P    ↓       ↓  P ↓   ↓  P  ↓    ↓   P  ↓↓

        D(2)                        G(2)
        Goin'  to Mon - ta-na just to throw  the houl-i-han,  they
        P    ↓    ↓      P ↓ ↓       P   ↓    ↓     P  ↓↓

        D(2)                        G(2)
        Feed   in the  coul-ees, they wa - ter in the  draw,    their
        P    ↓ ↓        P   ↓  ↓     P  ↓    ↓     P  ↓↓

        D(2)                    C(1)      G(1)
        Tails   are all  mat-ted,   their backs are all raw.
        P    ↓   ↓ P    ↓↓      P    ↓  ↓ P    ↓

        G        D(2)                    G(2)
Chorus: Ride a-round,   lit-tle do-gies, ride a - round    them slow,
        ↓    ↓ P  ↓↓    P ↓  ↓       P   ↓↓        P   ↓

                 D(2)                C(1)      G(1)
        For they're fi-er-y  and  snuff-y and rar-in' to go.
        ↓         P ↓↓   P    ↓↓ P ↓ ↓ P    ↓   ↓
```

2.   Old Bill Jones had two daughters and a song,
      One went to Denver, the other went wrong.
      His wife, she died in a poolroom fight
      But still he keeps singing from morning to night:

3.   When I die, take my saddle from the wall
      And put it on my pony, and lead him from his stall;
      Tie my bones to his back, turn our faces to the west
      And we'll ride the prairies that we love the best.

❖³² THE ITSY BITSY SPIDER

Horseback Strum, playfully
Chords: SmartStart G, Easy D
Beginning Singing Note: D, 4th string, open
Capo Position: 5th fret

Traditional Melody
New Lyrics by Jessica Baron Turner

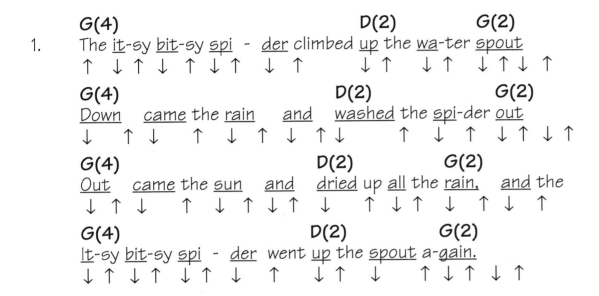

2. The creepy crawly earth worm is hiding underground
    Now he pops his head up to take a look around
    He takes a bath in raindrops, shakes them off and then,
    The creepy crawly earth worm goes underground again.

3. The rolly pole-y sow bug is rocking on her back
    Now she's rolling over to find a tasty snack
    She crawls inside an apple, crunch, crunch, crunch
    And she calls to all her children, "Come on, it's time for lunch!"

Science Activity: Invite children to spend several minutes outside observing any living creatures they can see. They can do this alone or in pairs.

Langauge Arts Activity: Teach children to write creatively and rhyme when they create new verses about the animals and insects they've seen, and these creatures' habits. The first and second lines end in one rhyme scheme and the third and fourth lines end in a different one. This form in music is called "A-A-B-B."

❸❸ JINGLE BELLS

Marching Strum or Two Step Strum
Chords: SmartStart G, Easy D, Easy C
First Singing Note: D, 4th string, open
Capo Position: 7th fret

By James Pierpont, 1857

G(4)
1. Dash-ing through the snow   on a
   P   ↓   P   ↓   P ↓   P   ↓

G(2)   C(2)   D(4)
One-horse o-pen sleigh,   O'er the fields we go,
 P   ↓   P ↓ P   ↓P↓ P   ↓   P   ↓ P ↓ P ↓

D(2)   G(6)
Laugh-ing all the way;   Bells on bob-tails ring,
P   ↓ P↓ P ↓ P ↓ P   ↓ P ↓ P ↓ P ↓

G(2)   C(2)   D(2)   G(2)
Mak-ing spir-its bright,   what fun it is to ride and sing a
P   ↓ P ↓ P   ↓ P ↓   P ↓ P↓ P ↓ P   ↓

D(2)   G(1)   D(1)
Sleigh-ing song to-night,   oh...
P   ↓ P   ↓ P   ↓ P   ↓

G(8)
Chorus: Jin-gle bells, jin-gle bells, jin-gle all the way!
 P ↓ P   ↓ P ↓ P   ↓ P↓ P ↓ P ↓ P ↓

C(2)   G(2)   D(4)
O' what fun it is to ride in a one-horse o-pen sleigh. Hey!
P ↓   P ↓P↓ P ↓ P ↓   P↓ P ↓ P ↓

G(8)
Jin-gle bells, jin-gle bells,   jin-gle all the way!
P ↓ P   ↓ P ↓ P   ↓ P↓ P ↓ P ↓ P ↓

C(2)   G(2)   D(2)   G(2)
O' what fun it is to ride in a one-horse o-pen sleigh.
P ↓   P ↓P↓ P ↓ P ↓   P↓ P ↓ P ↓

36

2. A day or two ago, I thought I'd take a ride,
    And soon Miss Fanny Bright was seated by my side;
    The horse was lean and lank; Misfortune seemed his lot;
    He got into a drifted bank, and we, we got upsot.

3. A day or two ago, the story I must tell
    I went out on the snow and on my back I fell;
    A gent was riding by in a one-horse open sleigh,
    He laughed as there I sprawling lie, but quickly drove away.

4. Now the ground is white. Go it while you're young,
    Take the girls tonight and sing this sleighing song;
    Just get a bob-tailed bay two-forty as his speed
    Hitch him to an open sleigh and crack! you'll take the lead.

◆34 **JOHN HENRY**

Traditional

Two Step Strum, emphasis on the backbeat
Chords: SmartStart G, Easy D
First Singing Note: D, 1st string, open
Capo Position: None

 D(1)   G(7)
1.   We-ell,   ev - 'ry   Mon - day   morn-ing
     P ↓   P ↓ P ↓ P   ↓ P ↓ P   ↓   P ↓ P ↓

 G(5)   D(3)
 When the blue - birds be-gin to   sing
     P   ↓ P ↓ P   ↓ P ↓ P ↓ P ↓ P ↓ P ↓

 D(1)   G(8)
 You can see   John   Hen - ry   out on   the line,   you can
     P ↓   P ↓ P ↓ P ↓ P ↓ P ↓ P↓ P ↓ P ↓

 G(7)
 Hear   John   Hen-ry's ham-mer ring, Lord,   Lord!
     P ↓ P ↓ P   ↓   P   ↓ P ↓ P ↓ P ↓

 G(3)   D(2)   G(3)
 You can hear   John   Hen-ry's   ham-mer   ring.
     P ↓   P ↓ P ↓ P   ↓   P   ↓   P ↓ P ↓ P ↓

2.   When John Henry was a little baby sittin' on his Daddy's knee
       He picked up a hammer and a little piece of steel
       Said, "Hammer's gonna be the death of me, Lord, Lord...
       Said, "Hammer's gonna be the death of me."

3.   Well the captain said to John Henry, "Gonna bring me a steam drill 'round.
       Gonna bring me a steam drill out on the job,
       Gonna whup that steel on down, Lord, Lord...
       Gonna whup that steel on down."

4.   John Henry said to his captain, "A man ain't nothin' but a man,
       And before I let that steam drill beat me down
       I'll die with that hammer in my hand, Lord, Lord...
       I'll die with that hammer in my hand."

5.   John Henry said to his shaker, "Shaker, why don't you pray?"
     "Cause if I miss this little piece of steel,
     Tomorrow be your buryin' day, Lord, Lord...
     Tomorrow be your buryin' day."

6.   John Henry was driving on the mountain and his hammer was flashing fire.
     The last words I ever heard that big man say,
     "Gimme a cool drink of water 'fore I die, Lord, Lord...
     Gimme a cool drink of water 'fore I die."

7.   John Henry he drove fifteen feet. the steam drill only made nine.
     But he hammered so hard that he broke his poor heart..
     So he laid down his hammer and died, Lord, Lord...
     Laid down his hammer and died.

8.   They took John Henry to the graveyard. and they buried him in the sand.
     And every locomotive that comes roaring right on by
     Says, "There lies a steel drivin' man, Lord, Lord...
     There lies a steel drivin' man."

☆ JOHNNY HAS GONE FOR A SOLDIER

Marching Strum or Boom-Chicka Strum, slowly
Chords: Em, Intermediate D, Easy C
Beginning Singing Note: G, 1st string, 5th fret
Capo Position: None

Traditional

This song was brought to America by immigrants from Ireland during the 1700s. It became very popular during the Revolutionary War, and speaks of the sadness felt by every soldier's sweetheart.

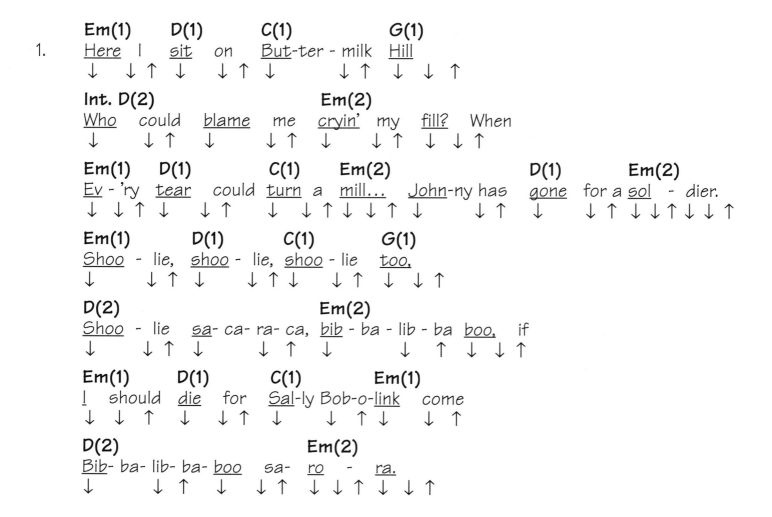

2.   I'd sell my clock, I'd sell my reel, likewise sell my spinning wheel
     to buy my love a sword of steel, Johnny has gone for a soldier

3.   Me oh my, I loved him so. Broke my heart to see him go,
     And only time will heal my woe; Johnny has gone for a soldier.

◆ LAS MAÑANITAS

Three Step Strum or Waltz Strum
Chords: SmartStart G, Easy D, Easy C
First Singing Note: D, 4th string, open
Capo Position: 3rd fret

Traditional Mexican Birthday Song

```
G(1)                          D(1)            G(1)              C(1)
    Es-tas son    las ma-ña-ni - tas que can-ta - ba   el Rey Da-vid
 ↓          P ↓    ↓   P ↓    ↓    P ↓        ↓   P ↓

C          G(2)
Hoy por ser di - a de tu san - to, te las can-
 ↓          P ↓   ↓    P    ↓    ↓

D(1)     G(1)      D(1)                G(1)
-ta-mos a ti.    Des- pi-er-ta, mi bi-en des-pi-er-ta
 P ↓    ↓P↓↓ P ↓      ↓        ↓      P      ↓

   D(1)                 G(1)
Mi-ra    que ya a-man-e-ci-o. Ya los
↓ P     ↓       ↓    P ↓ ↓

C(1)        G(1)           D(1)     G(1)
pa - ja- rill-os can-tan, la lu-na ya  se me-ti-o.
 P ↓   ↓   P ↓       ↓    P ↓ ↓ P   ↓ ↓
```

41

⬦ LINCOLN AND LIBERTY

Waltz Strum, Three Step Strum or Marching Strum

Chords: SmartStart G, Easy D, Easy C, Em
Beginning Singing Note: D, 1st string, open
Capo Position: 3rd fret

Traditional

This song was written by citizens who wanted Abe Lincoln to be elected President of the United States. The song refers to Kentucky, Lincoln's home state, Indiana where he lived for a time, and Illinois, known long ago for its large population of "sucker" fish. Illinois is the state where Lincoln practiced law and began his rise to power.

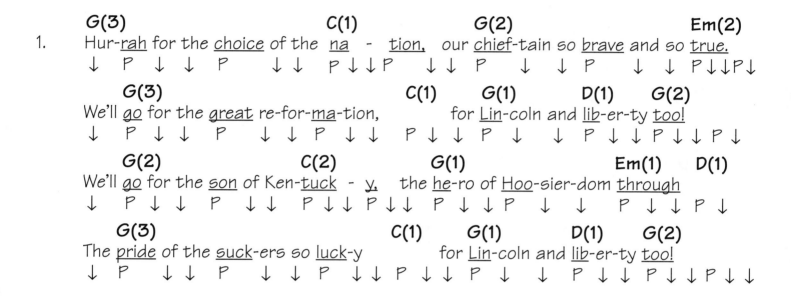

```
         G(3)                        C(1)           G(2)                 Em(2)
1.   Hur-rah for the choice of the  na  -  tion,  our chief-tain so brave and so true.
      ↓  P  ↓  ↓  P     ↓ ↓  P↓↓P   ↓ ↓  P   ↓  ↓ P    ↓  ↓ P↓↓P↓

         G(3)                          C(1)    G(1)      D(1)    G(2)
     We'll go for the great re-for-ma-tion,        for Lin-coln and lib-er-ty too!
      ↓  P  ↓  ↓   P    ↓  ↓  P  ↓ ↓   P ↓ ↓ P ↓   ↓  P ↓ ↓ P↓↓P↓

         G(2)                 C(2)          G(1)                  Em(1)     D(1)
     We'll go for the son of Ken-tuck - y,   the he-ro of Hoo-sier-dom through
      ↓  P ↓ ↓   P   ↓ ↓   P↓↓P↓↓  P ↓ ↓ P   ↓   ↓    P ↓ ↓ P ↓

         G(3)                          C(1)    G(1)      D(1)    G(2)
     The pride of the suck-ers so luck-y        for Lin-coln and lib-er-ty too!
      ↓ P   ↓ ↓  P   ↓  ↓ P  ↓ ↓ P↓↓ P ↓   ↓  P ↓ ↓ P↓↓P↓↓
```

2.   We'll find what by felling and mauling, our rail-splitter statesman can do.
     For the people are everywhere calling for Lincoln and liberty too!
     Then up with the banner so glorious, the star spangled red, white and blue.
     We'll fight til our banner's victorious for Lincoln and liberty too!

42

◆38 LOOBY LU (HERE WE GO)

Horseback Strum
Chords: SmartStart G, Easy D
Beginning Singing Note: G, 3rd string, open
Capo Position: 3rd fret

Traditional

Chorus:

G(6) Here we go loo-by lu   D(2) Here we go loo-by lie
↓   ↑ ↓ ↑ ↓ ↑ ↓ ↑ ↓   ↑ ↓ ↑ ↓ ↑ ↓ ↑

G(4) Here we go loo-by lu   D(2) all on a Sat-ur-day G(2) night You
↓   ↑ ↓ ↑ ↓ ↑ ↓ ↑ ↓ ↑   ↓   ↑ ↓ ↑ ↓ ↑

1.

G(6) Put your left hand in,   you take your left hand out   D(2) You
↓ ↑ ↓ ↑ ↓ ↑ ↓ ↑ ↓ ↑ ↓ ↑ ↓ ↑ ↓ ↑

G(4) Give your hand a shake, shake, shake and
↓ ↑ ↓ ↑ ↓ ↑ ↓ ↑

D(2) Turn your-self a - G(2) bout!
↓ ↑ ↓ ↑ ↓ ↑ ↓ ↑

2.   You put your right hand in...

3.   You put your left foot in...

4.   You put your right foot in...

5.   You put your whole self in...

Group Movement Activity: Invite children to form a circle and follow the directions in the song by placing their hands, feet, etc. into the center of the circle while they sing, then turning around in place. Together, you can make up new verses to help young children learn the names for many parts of their bodies.

Bilingual Activity: This song lends itself beautifully to teaching children the same words in Spanish or any other language.

🔷³⁹ MAMA DON'T ALLOW

Boom-Chicka Strum, energetically
Chords: SmartStart G, Easy D, Easy C
First Singing Note: G, 3rd string, open
Capo Position: 7th fret

Traditional

1.
G(8)
Ma-ma don't al-<u>low</u> no   <u>mu</u>-sic   <u>play</u>-ing 'round   <u>here!</u>
↓   ↓   ↑↓↓↑↓ ↓↑↓   ↓   ↑↓↓↑↓↓↑↓↓↑↓↓↑

G(4)   **D(4)**
Ma-ma don't al-<u>low</u> no   <u>mu</u>-sic   <u>play</u>-ing 'round   <u>here!</u>
↓   ↓   ↑↓↓↑ ↓ ↓↑↓   ↓   ↑↓↓↑↓↓↑↓↓↑↓↓↑

G(4)
<u>We</u> don't   <u>care</u> what   <u>Ma</u>-ma don't al-<u>low…</u>
↓ ↓ ↑ ↓ ↓ ↓ ↑ ↓   ↓   ↑ ↓ ↓ ↑

C(4)
<u>Gon</u>-na make   <u>mu</u>-sic   <u>an</u>-y   -   <u>how!</u>
↓   ↓   ↑↓ ↓↑↓↓ ↑   ↓↓↑

G(2)   **D(2)**   **G(4)**
Ma-ma don't al-<u>low</u> no   <u>mu</u>-sic   <u>play</u>-ing 'round   <u>here!</u>
↓   ↓   ↑↓↓↑↓ ↓↑↓   ↓   ↑ ↓↓↑↓↓↑↓↓↑↓↓↑

Rhythm Jam Session: Everybody sits in a circle, holding a musical instrument. For each new verse, you can add the name of the next person in the circle and the instrument he or she is playing. Example: Sarah don't allow no bell playing around here…etc.)

Social Skills Songwriting: Turn this into a fun way to remember class rules or good manners…Teacher don't allow no "pushin' and shovin'" or "cheatin' eyes" around here, and put unacceptable behaviors into a funny, healthy context.

◆ MARY HAD A BABY

Traditional,
from South Carolina, 1800s

Two Step Strum, walking pace
Chords: SmartStart G, Easy D, Easy C
First Singing Note: G, 3rd string, open
Capo Position: 5th fret

This beautifully told story is an easy Christmas carol for young children to sing, remember, and enjoy. To emphasize the backbeat, play each down strum a little more energetically than you do each bass note.

```
        G(2)                    C(1)    D(1)
1.   Mar-y  had a  ba - by.  Aye,   Lord
     P        ↓      P    ↓    P   ↓   P    ↓

        G(2)                    C(1)      D(1)
     Mar-y  had a  ba- by.   Aye, my   Lord
     P        ↓      P    ↓    P    ↓     P     ↓

        G(2)                    C(2)
     Mar-y  had a  ba - by.  Aye, my  Lord.      The
     P        ↓      P    ↓    P    ↓    P      ↓

        G(2)                         D(1)      G(1)
     Peo-ple keep a-com-in' but the  train  has  gone.
     P        ↓      P         ↓      P    ↓   P    ↓
```

2.   Where did she lay him? Aye, Lord…

3.   Laid him in a manger. Aye, Lord…

4.   What did she name him? Aye, Lord…

5.   Named him King Jesus. Aye, Lord…

6.   Who heard the singing? Aye, Lord…

7.   The shepherds heard the singing! Aye, Lord, etc.

8.   The star keeps a-shining. Aye, Lord…

9.   Jesus went to Egypt. Aye, Lord…

10.   Travel on a donkey. Aye, Lord…

11.   Angels went around him. Aye, Lord, etc.

❹ MICHAEL ROW YOUR BOAT ASHORE

Marching Strum or Cowboy Strum
Chords: SmartStart G, Easy D, Easy C
First Singing Note: D, 3rd string, open
Capo Position: 3rd fret

Traditional

Chorus:

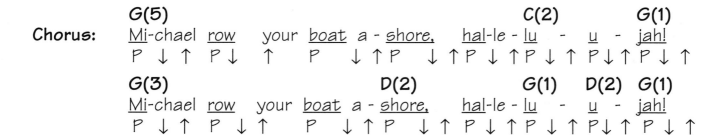

1. Sister helped to trim the sail, hallalujah (repeat)

2. River Jordan is muddy and cold, hallalujah /Chills the body but not the soul

3. River Jordan is deep and wide, hallalujah /Milk and honey on the other side

✪ OATS, PEAS, BEANS AND BARLEY GROWS

Horseback Strum
Chords: SmartStart G, Easy D, Easy C, Em
First Singing Note: B, 2nd string, open
Capo Position: 3rd fret

Traditional

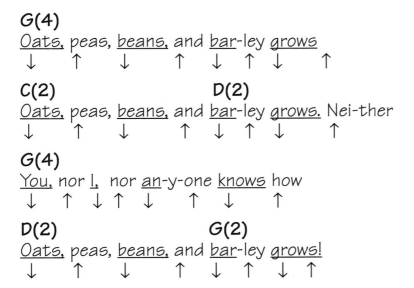

G(4)
<u>Oats,</u> peas, <u>beans,</u> and <u>bar</u>-ley <u>grows</u>
↓   ↑   ↓   ↑   ↓ ↑ ↓   ↑

C(2)   **D(2)**
<u>Oats,</u> peas, <u>beans,</u> and <u>bar</u>-ley <u>grows.</u> Nei-ther
↓   ↑   ↓   ↑   ↓ ↑ ↓   ↑

G(4)
<u>You,</u> nor <u>I,</u> nor <u>an</u>-y-one <u>knows</u> how
↓   ↑   ↓ ↑ ↓   ↑   ↓   ↑

D(2)   **G(2)**
<u>Oats,</u> peas, <u>beans,</u> and <u>bar</u>-ley <u>grows!</u>
↓   ↑   ↓   ↑   ↓ ↑ ↓ ↑

Songwriting and Science Activity: What other living things grow? In a forest or jungle? In a desert? Invite children to make up their own verses about plants, flowers, and trees, or even animals!

THE OLD CHISHOLM TRAIL

Horseback Strum, Two Step Strum, or Cowboy Strum
Chords: SmartStart G, Easy D, Easy C
First Singing Note: G, 3rd string, open
Capo Position: 3rd fret

Traditional Melody
Lyrics Adapted by Jessica Baron Turner

G(4)
1. Come a-long   boys and   lis-ten to my   tale and I'll
    P   ↓ ↑   P   ↓ ↑ P   ↓ ↑   P   ↓   ↑

D(2)   **G(2)**
Tell you all my troub-les on the Old Chis-holm Trail, come a-
P   ↓ ↑ P   ↓ ↑ P ↓   ↑   P   ↓   ↑

Chorus:

D(2)   **G(2)**
-ti- yi   yip-pee yip-pee   yay yip-pee yay, come a-
P ↓ ↑ P   ↓ ↑   P ↓ ↑   P   ↓   ↑

D(2)   **G(2)**
-ti- yi   yip-pee yip-pee   yay   2. On a
P ↓ ↑ P   ↓ ↑   P ↓ ↑ P   ↓ ↑

2. (On a) ten dollar horse and a forty dollar saddle, I
    Started out a-punchin' them long horned cattle.

3. (I'm) up in the mornin' 'fore day-light, and be-
    'Fore I get to sleepin the moon's shining bright.

4. (It's) bacon and beans almost every single day
    Oh, I'd sooner be spoonin' down some dry prairie hay.

5. (I) went to the boss for to draw my "role"
    He had it figured out I was nine dollars in the hole.

6. (So I) went up to the boss and said, "I won't take that!"
    And I popped him in the kisser with my old slouch hat.

7. (I'l) sell my outfit soon as I can, 'cause I
    Ain't punchin' cattle for no mean boss man.

8. (With my) knees in the saddle and my seat in the sky, I'll
    Quit punchin' cattle in the sweet by 'n by.

Note: The lyrics in parentheses are sung on the downbeat with a D chord.

◆ OLD DAN TUCKER

Marching Strum or Two Step Strum, Walking Pace
By Dan Emmett
Chords: SmartStart G, Easy D, Easy C
First Singing Note: B, 2nd string, open
Capo Position: 5th fret

This song was written in the 1800s by Dan Emmett, a 15 year old songwriter who was a drummer-fifer in the regular army at the Newport Barracks in Kentucky.

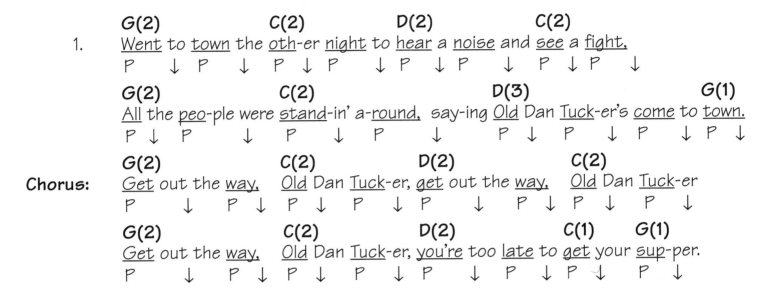

2. Old Dan Tucker's a fine old man,
   Washed his face in fryin' pan.
   Combed his hair with a wagon wheel,
   And died with a toothache in his heel. (Chorus)

3. Old Dan Tucker come to town,
   Ridin' a billygoat, leading' a hound.
   Houndog barked and the billygoat jumped,
   Throwed Old Dan right straddle of a stump. (Chorus)

4. Old Dan Tucker climbed a tree,
   His Lord and Master for to see.
   The limb, it broke and Dan did fall,
   Never saw his Lord at all. (Chorus)

5. Old Dan Tucker come to town,
   Swingin' the ladies 'round and 'round.
   First to the right and then to the left,
   And then to the one you love the best. (Chorus)

45 OVER THE RIVER AND THROUGH THE WOODS

Horseback Strum, brightly
Chords: SmartStart G, Easy D, Easy C
First Singing Note: D, 1st string, open
Capo Position: 3rd fret

Traditional

This song began as a poem written by Lydia Maria Child. It was published in 1844 in Flowers for Children, Vol. 2.

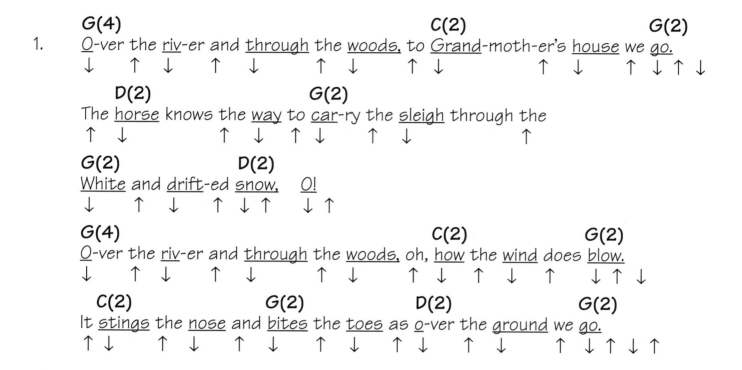

1.
G(4)   C(2)   G(2)

O-ver the riv-er and through the woods, to Grand-moth-er's house we go.
↓   ↑ ↓   ↑ ↓   ↑ ↓   ↑ ↓   ↑ ↓   ↑ ↓↑↓

         D(2)   G(2)

The horse knows the way to car-ry the sleigh through the
↑ ↓   ↑ ↓ ↑↓   ↑ ↓   ↑

G(2)   D(2)

White and drift-ed snow,   O!
↓   ↑ ↓   ↑ ↓↑   ↓↑

G(4)   C(2)   G(2)

O-ver the riv-er and through the woods, oh, how the wind does blow.
↓   ↑ ↓   ↑ ↓   ↑ ↓   ↑ ↓ ↑ ↓ ↑   ↓↑↓

     C(2)   G(2)   D(2)   G(2)

It stings the nose and bites the toes as o-ver the ground we go.
↑↓   ↑ ↓   ↑ ↓   ↑ ↓   ↑ ↓   ↑ ↓   ↑ ↓↑↓↑

2.   Over the river and through the woods. Trot fast my dapple gray.
Spring over the ground like a hunting hound on this Thanksgiving Day,
Hey! Over the river and through the woods, now Grandmother's face I spy.
Hurrah for the fun, is the pudding done? Hurrah for the pumpkin pie.

◆46 THE RIDDLE SONG

Horseback Strum or Cowboy Strum, gently   Traditional
Chords: SmartStart G, Easy D, Easy C
First Singing Note: D, 4th string, open
Capo Position: 5th fret

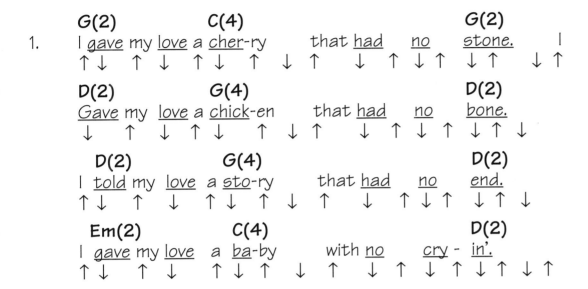

2.   How can there be a cherry that had no stone?
       How can there be a chicken that had no bone?
       How can there be a story that had no end?
       How can there be a a baby with no cryin'?

3.   A cherry, when it's bloomin', it has no stone.
       A chicken, when it's piping, it has no bone.
       The story that I love you, it has no end.

       Em(1)   **C(1)**   **D(1)**   **G(1)**
       A ba-by, when it's sleep-ing, has no cry-in'.

Quiet Time Activity: When children would benefit from hearing soothing music, such as winding-down time or recovering from a traumatic event, singing this song can, as it has for many decades, bring them comfort.

◆47 SHENANDOAH

Marching Strum, gently
Chords: SmartStart G, Easy D, Easy C, Em
First Singing Note: D, 4th string, open
Capo Position: 3rd fret

Traditional

Shenandoah, meaning "daughter of the stars" is the name of a river and a valley in Shenandoah, as well a person. The singer, a fur trader, must leave his true love, the daughter of Algonquin chief Shenandoah and cross the Missouri River.

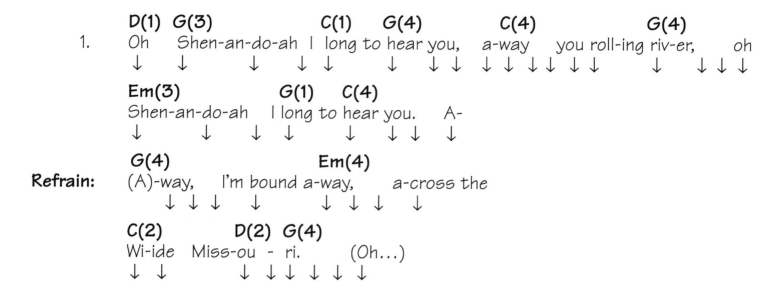

2. Oh Shenandoah, I love your daughter, away, you rolling river..
   For her I've crossed the rolling water.

3. This trader loves an Indian maiden, away you rolling river.
   With notions this canoe is laden.

4. Oh, Shenandoah, I'm bound to leave you, away you rolling river!
   Oh, Shenandoah, I'll not deceive you.

5. Oh, Shenandoah, I long to see you, away you rolling river.
   Oh, Shenandoah, I long to see you.

48 SIMPLE GIFTS

Marching Strum, gently
Chords: SmartStart G, Easy D, Easy C
First Singing Note: D, 4th string, open
Capo Position: 5th fret

Traditional Shaker Hymn

G(12)
          'Tis a gift to be sim-ple, 'tis a gift to be free. 'Tis a
↓ ↓ ↓ ↓   ↓   ↓   ↓   ↓   ↓   ↓   ↓   ↓

D(8)
Gift to come down where we ought to be. And
↓ ↓ ↓   ↓   ↓   ↓   ↓ ↓

G(8)
When we find our-selves in the place just right, we will
↓   ↓   ↓   ↓   ↓   ↓   ↓   ↓

D(4)   C(2)   G(2)
Be in the val-ley of love and de-light
↓ ↓   ↓   ↓   ↓   ↓   ↓   ↓

G(8)
When   true   sim-pli-ci-ty is gained, to
↓ ↓ ↓   ↓   ↓   ↓   ↓   ↓

G(4)   D(4)
Bow and to bend we will not be a-shamed, to
↓   ↓   ↓   ↓   ↓   ↓   ↓   ↓   ↓

G(8)
Turn, to turn will be our de-light 'til by
↓ ↓   ↓   ↓ ↓ ↓   ↓   ↓

D(4)   C(2)   G(2)
Turn-ing, turn-ing, we come a-round right.
↓   ↓   ↓   ↓   ↓   ↓   ↓   ↓

◆⁴⁹ SKIP TO MY LOU

Marching Strum, Horseback Strum, or Two Step Strum
Chords: SmartStart G, Easy D
First Singing Note: B, 2nd string, open
Capo Position: 5th fret

Traditional Melody
Additional Lyrics by Jessica Baron Turner

Chorus:

G(4)   D(4)
<u>Skip,</u> <u>skip,</u> <u>skip</u> to my <u>Lou,</u> <u>skip,</u> <u>skip,</u> <u>skip</u> to my <u>Lou</u>
P ↓ P ↓ P ↓   P ↓ P ↓ P ↓ P   ↓   P ↓

G(4)   D(2)   G(2)
<u>Skip,</u> <u>skip,</u> <u>skip</u> to my <u>Lou,</u> <u>Skip</u> to my <u>Lou</u> my <u>dar</u> - <u>lin'</u>
P ↓ P ↓ P ↓   P ↓ P   ↓   P ↓ P ↓ P ↓

1. Cows in the pasture moo to my Lou,
    Cows in the pasture moo to my Lou
    Cows in the pasture moo to my Lou
    Moo to my Lou my darlin'
    Walk, walk, walk to my Lou, Walk, walk, walk to my Lou
    Walk, walk, walk to my Lou, Walk to my Lou my darlin'

2. Horses in the meadow neigh to my Lou. Run, run, run...

3. Dogs in the barnyard bark to my Lou. Jump, jump, jump...

4. Cats on the front porch mew to my Lou. Stretch, stretch, stretch....

Movement and Music Activity: This is an easy circle time or physical education activity for young children. Invite everyone to make a circle and stand up, holding hands. Begin singing the lyrics while everyone moves according to the directions in the song.

Songwriting Activity: For a lively discussion, ask children to name different animals and show and tell the class how the animals move. Now you can add their ideas to the song. Everybody will want a turn!

⬦ SLOOP JOHN B.

Two Step Strum or **Cowboy Strum**

Traditional, New England

Chords: SmartStart G, Easy D, Easy C
First Singing Note: D , 4th string, open
Capo Position: 5th fret

This song was written over a hundred years ago, supposedly in New England, but it refers to a young sailor's unbearable first trip to the Bahamas.

G(8)
1. We come on the sloop John B.　　My grand - fath-er and me.
        P　　↓↑　P　　↓↑P↓↑P↓↑　P　　↓↑P　　↓↑　P↓↑P↓↑

G(4)　　　　　　　　　　　　　　　　　　D(3)
'Round　　Nas-sau　town　　we did　go.
        P　↓↑　P　↓↑　P　↓↑P　↓↑　P↓↑P↓ ↑P↓↑

D(1)　　　　G(4)　　　　　　　　　　　　　　C(4)
Drink-ing all　night　　　　　　Got in-to a　fight　　　　　|
        P　　↓↑P↓↑P↓↑P ↓↑ P　↓↑　P↓↑P↓↑P↓↑P↓↑

G(2)　　　　　　　D(2)　　　　　　　G(4)
Feel so　break-up　　I want　to go home.
        P　↓↑P　↓↑　P↓↑　P　↓↑P↓↑P↓↑P↓↑P

G(8)
Chorus: So hoist up the John B. sails.　　See how the main-sail sets.
        ↓↑P　↓↑P ↓↑P↓↑P↓↑P　↓↑P　↓↑P↓↑P↓↑

G(4)　　　　　　　　　　　　　　　　　　D(3)
Send for the Cap-tain a - shore,　let me go　home.
        P　↓↑　P　↓↑P　↓↑P　↓↑　P↓↑P↓↑P↓↑

D(1)　　　G(4)　　　　　　　　　　　C(4)
Let me go　home.　　　　Let me go　home.　　　　|
        P　↓↑P↓↑P↓↑P↓↑ P　↓↑P↓↑P↓↑P↓↑P↓↑

G(2)　　　　　　　D(2)　　　　　G(4)
Feel so　break - up,　　| want to go　home.
        P↓↑P　↓↑　P↓↑P　↓↑P↓↑P↓↑P↓↑P↓↑

2. The first mate he got drunk. Broke up the people's trunk.
    Constable had to come and take me away.
    Sheriff Johnstone, please leave me alone.
    I feel so break-up, I want to go home.

3. The poor cook he got fits. Threw away all the grits.
    Then he took and ate up all of my corn.
    Let me go home. I want to go home.
    I feel so break-up, I want to go home.

◆ SWING LOW SWEET CHARIOT

Horseback Strum

Traditional

Chords: SmartStart G, Easy D, Easy C, Em optional

First Singing Note: B, 2nd string, open

Capo Position: 5th fret

Strumming Clue: Because the lyrics of this song move so slowly, each syllable receives a full down and up Horseback Strum.

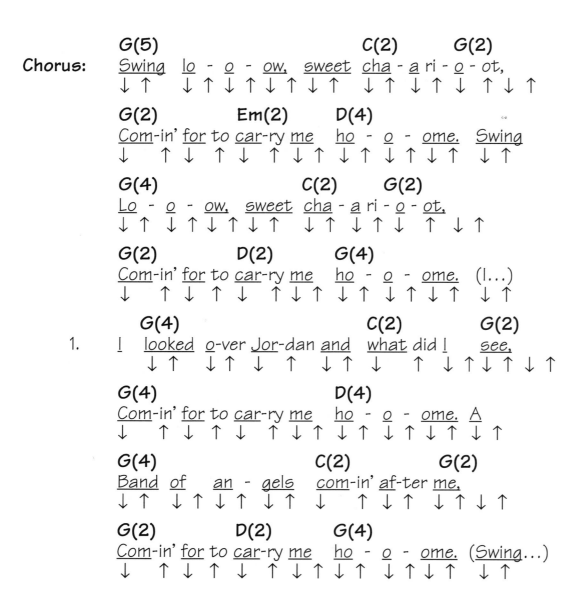

2.   If you get there before I do, comin' for to carry me home
      Tell all my people I'm comin' there too.

❖ THESE ARE THE COLORS I KNOW

Three Step Strum
Chords: SmartStart G, Easy D, Easy C
First Singing Note: G, 3rd string, open
Capo Position: 2nd fret

Based on "Chiapanecas"
New Lyrics by Jessica Baron Turner

1.
    G(2)   D(2)
    Red is a col-or I know. Ro-jo!
    P ↓ ↓ P ↓↓P ↓ ↓ P ↓ ↓

    D(2)   G(2)
    Red as the roos-ters that crow. Ro-jo! In
    P ↓ ↓ P ↓ ↓ P ↓ ↓ P↓↓

    G(2)   D(2)
    Span-ish we call it ro-jo. Ro-jo!
    P   ↓ ↓ P ↓↓P↓↓ P ↓ ↓

    D(2)   G(2)
    Red is a col-or I know. Ro-jo!
    P ↓↓P ↓↓P ↓ ↓ P ↓ ↓

Chorus:
    C(4)   G(4)
    Red,   red,   red is a col-or, bold - er   than ev'-ry oth-er.
    P ↓ ↓ P ↓ ↓ P ↓↓ P ↓↓P↓↓ P↓↓P ↓↓ P ↓ ↓ P ↓ ↓

    D(4)   G(1)   D(1)   G(2)
    Red,   red,   red is a col-or, in Span-ish we call it ro-jo! Ro-jo!
    P ↓ ↓ P ↓↓ P ↓↓ P ↓ ↓ P ↓ ↓ P   ↓ ↓ P ↓ ↓ P ↓↓P↓↓

2.   White is a color I know. Blanco! White as the tortilla dough. Blanco!
      In Spanish we call it "blanco." Blanco! White is a color I know. Blanco!

Chorus: White, white, white is a color, brighter than any other.
      White, white, white is a color,
      In Spanish we call it "blanco"! Blanco!
      Red, red, red,...

3.   Green is a color we say "verde." Green as the chiles in May. Verde!
      In Spanish we call it "verde." Verde! Green is a color we say "verde."

Chorus: Green, green, green is a color, fresher than every other.
      Green, green, green is a color,
      In Spanish we call it "verde"! Verde!
      White, white, white, etc., then Red, red, red,...

Final Chorus: Red, white, and green are the colors,
      Waving like sisters and brothers.
      Red, white, and green are the colors, on the flag of Mexico.
      Rojo, blanco, verde, olé!

✦ TELL ME WHY

Waltz Strum or Three Step Strum, gently
Chords: SmartStart G, Easy C, Easy D, A
First Singing Note: D, 4th string, open
Capo Position: 5th fret

Traditional Melody
New Lyrics by Jessica Baron Turner

```
       D(1)      G(1)       C(1)       G(2)
1.  Te-ell me why - y  the stars    do shine.
    P  ↓  ↓  P  ↓  ↓  P  ↓   ↓ P  ↓   ↓ P ↓ ↓

       D(1)      G(1)         C(1)      D(2)
    Te-ell me why - y the  i - i - vy twines.
    P  ↓  ↓ P    ↓ ↓  P ↓  ↓  P  ↓   ↓ P ↓ ↓

       D(1)      G(1)        C(1)        G(1)
    Te-ell me why-y the skies    are  blue,
    P  ↓ ↓  P  ↓ ↓  P  ↓  ↓   P   ↓    ↓

    G(1)      C(1)        D(1)       G(1)
    And I  will tell you just why I love you.
    P   ↓ ↓ P ↓  ↓  P  ↓ ↓ P   ↓    ↓
```

2. Because God made the stars to shine
    Because God made the ivy twine
    Because God made the skies so blue
    Because God made you, that's why I love you

3. Tell me why night turns to morn
    Tell me why each baby is born
    Tell me why each breath is new
    And I will tell you just why I love you

4. Because God made the sun above
    Because God made us all from love
    Because God made my dream come true
    Because God made you, that's why I love you

🔶54 **THE WASSAIL SONG**

Horseback Strum, lightly, into Marching Strum

Chords: SmartStart G, Easy D, Easy C, Em

First Singing Note: G, 3rd string, open

Capo Position: 3rd fret

Traditional English Christmas Carol

Quick Change Challenge: The chord changes in this song occur very quickly. Play this song without the words for a wonderful "Quick Change Challenge!" If you can do it smoothly, you are ready to move on to standard tuning.

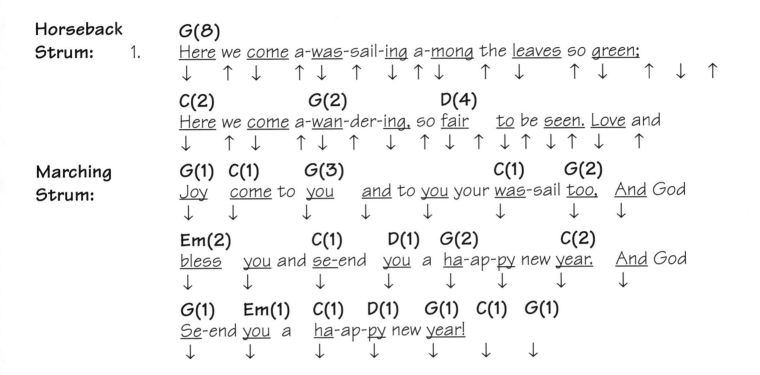

Horseback Strum:　1.

G(8)
Here we come a-was-sail-ing a-mong the leaves so green;
↓　↑　↓　↑ ↓　↑　↓ ↑↓　↑　↓　↑ ↓　↑　↓　↑

C(2)　　　　　　G(2)　　　　　　D(4)
Here we come a-wan-der-ing, so fair　to be seen. Love and
↓　↑　↓　↑ ↓　↑　↓　↑ ↓　↑ ↓↑ ↓ ↑ ↓　↑

Marching Strum:

G(1)　C(1)　　　G(3)　　　　　　　　C(1)　　G(2)
Joy　come to you　and to you your was-sail too,　And God
↓　　↓　　　　↓　　　↓　　　　↓　　　　↓　　　↓

Em(2)　　　　　C(1)　　D(1) G(2)　　　　　C(2)
bless　you and se-end　you a ha-ap-py new year.　And God
↓　　↓　　　↓　　　↓　　↓　　↓　　↓　　↓

G(1)　　Em(1)　C(1)　D(1)　G(1) C(1)　G(1)
Se-end you a　ha-ap-py new year!
↓　　　↓　　　↓　　↓　　↓　　↓　　↓

🎵 YANKEE DOODLE

Marching Strum or Two Step Strum
Chords: SmartStart G, Easy D, Easy C
First Singing Note: G, 3rd string, open
Capo Position: 7th fret

Traditional, Revolutionary War

1.
G(7)   D(1)
Fath-er and I went down to camp a-long with Cap-tain Good - ing;
↓   ↓   ↓   ↓   ↓   ↓   ↓   ↓

G(2)   C(2)   D(2)   G(2)
There we saw the men and boys as thick as hast-y pud - ding.
↓   ↓   ↓   ↓   ↓   ↓   ↓   ↓

Chorus:
C(4)   G(4)
Yan - kee doo-dle, keep it up, Yan - kee doo-dle dan - dy;
↓   ↓   ↓   ↓   ↓   ↓   ↓

C(4)   G(1)   D(1)   G(2)
Mind the mu-sic and the step, and with the girls be hand-y.
↓   ↓   ↓   ↓   ↓   ↓   ↓   ↓

2.   There was Captain Washington upon a slapping stallion,
A-giving orders to his men, I guess there was a million.
And then the feathers on his hat, they looked so' tarnal fin-a,
I wanted pockily to get to give to my Jemima.

3.   And then we saw a swamping gun, large as a log of maple;
Upon a deuced little cart, a load for father's cattle.
And every time they shoot it off, it takes a horn of powder;
It makes a noise like father's gun, only a nation louder.

4.   I went as nigh to one myself, as' Siah's underpinning;
And father went as nigh agin, I thought the deuce was in him.
We saw a little barrel, too, the heads were made of leather;
They knocked upon it with little clubs, and called the folks together.

5.   And there they'd fife away like fun, and play on cornstalk fiddles,
     And some had ribbons red as blood, all bound around their middles.
     The troopers, too, would gallop up and fire right in our faces;
     It scared me almost to death to see them run such races.

6.   Uncle Sam came there to change some pancakes and some onions,
     For lasses cake to carry home to give his wife and young ones.
     But I can't tell half I see they kept up such a smother;
     So I took my hat off, made a bow and scampered home to mother.

7.   Cousin Simon grew so bold, I thought he would have cocked it;
     I scared me so I streaked it off, and hung by father's pocket.
     And there I saw a pumpkin shell, as big as mother's basin;
     And every time they touched it off, they scampered like the nation.

ABOUT THE AUTHOR

Jessica Baron Turner is a teacher, musician, writer, and foremost, a mom. Children and adults love her work because it encourages them to learn at their own pace and follow their creative instincts. Like her co-authored 1995 award-winning book, Let's Make Music! (Hal Leonard Corporation), her best-selling method book SmartStart Guitar (Hal Leonard Corporation), provides simple step-by-step lessons that help beginners achieve success after success learning to play "by ear."

This SmartStart Guitar Songbook provides song arrangements based on Mrs. Turner's knowledge of learning styles and strategies. The arrangements in this book are designed to help beginners of all ages begin to hear, feel, and remember the music. These skills come most naturally to "auditory learners" who easily memorize what they hear. The songs in this book have been presented specially for "visual learners" who benefit from watching and reading whatever they are learning... even music made "by ear!"

Mrs. Turner holds a Bachelor of Arts degree in Child Development and a Masters degree in Clinical Psychology. She has been teaching guitar since 1974 and is currently working on bringing guitar education into public elementary school classrooms across the nation through "Guitars in the Classroom" a non-profit program under the auspices of the Community Music School in Santa Cruz, California. She lives with her husband, luthier Rick Turner, their son Elias, thirteen fish, two frogs and Frankie the Cat.

FOR ELIAS, WITH LOVE.

ACKNOWLEDGMENTS

Special thanks to The Old Town School of Folk Music in Chicago, Illinois for inspiration and valuable experiences, to all the great folk performers who've kept these songs fresh, David Lusterman and the folks at *Acoustic Guitar Magazine*, to Jeff Sultanof, Bill Walker, Justin Mayer, William Coulter, Brenda Hough and the teachers at Baldwin Elementary School and to teachers who devote themselves to care for kids each day, to the Los Angeles Public Library Main Branch and especially to my husband Rick for his steadfast belief in the importance of SmartStart Guitar, many, many thanks.